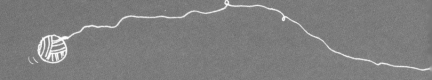

WHAT MAKES YOU

Smile?

- - - - - - - -

written by M.H. Clark

designed & illustrated by Joanna Price

COMPENDIUM™
INCORPORATED

With special thanks to: Jason Aldrich, Gerry Baird, Jay Baird, Neil Beaton, Josie Bissett, Laura Boro, Melissa Carlson, Tiffany Parente Connors, Jim & Alyssa Darragh & Family, Rob Estes, Pamela Farrington, Michael & Leianne Flynn & Family, Sarah Forster, Dan Harrill, Michael J. Hedge, Liz Heinlein & Family, Renee Holmes, Jennifer Hurwitz, Heidi Jones, Sheila Kamuda, Michelle Kim, Carol Anne Kennedy, June Martin, David Miller, Carin Moore, Moose, Josh Oakley, Jessica Phoenix & Tom DesLongchamp, Janet Potter & Family, Heidi & Jose Rodriguez, Diane Roger, Alie Satterlee, Kirsten & Garrett Sessions, Andrea Shirley, Jason Starling, Brien Thompson, Helen Tsao, Anne Whiting, Heidi Yamada & Family, Justi and Tote Yamada & Family, Bob and Val Yamada, Kaz & Kristin Yamada & Family, Tai & Joy Yamada, Anne Zadra, August & Arline Zadra, Dan Zadra and Gus & Rosie Zadra.

Written by M.H. Clark
Designed & Illustrated by Joanna Price

ISBN: 978-1-935414-09-4

First printing. Printed with soy ink in China.

> *You smile at life*
> *and it returns the smile.*
> — Ralph Ransom

Have you noticed? Our lives are filled with a wealth of everyday gifts: tiny moments, perfect little objects, and chance occurrences that add sparkle and joy to the everyday, if only we stop to appreciate them.

No matter where we are or what we are doing, these small wonders appear here and there like little exclamation points. They lift your spirits and renew your energy. They make every day into a treasure hunt. They put a smile on your face.

The best part? The little things that make life worth living are not expensive or difficult to see or hard to come by: a cup of tea with a friend. Homemade cookies. Clean sheets. A phone call from someone you love. Knowing you've done your best. When you start counting them all up, you realize that the little things aren't so little after all.

This book is a gift and a reminder. It's just the beginning of a list of the things that might make you smile. So go ahead, start reading. Start your own list. What makes you smile?

- - - - - - - - - -
new notebooks
- - - - - - - - -

making someone's day

homemade cookies

kids' lemonade stands

slumber parties

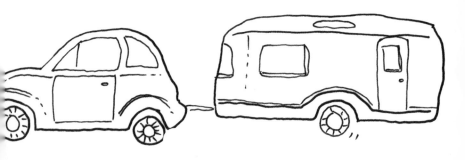

road trips

possibilities

perfect timing

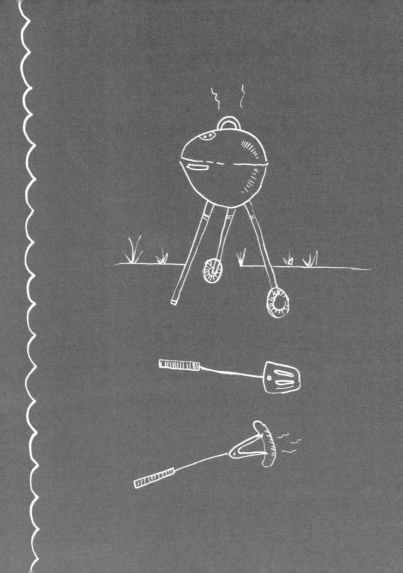

long weekends

candlelit dinners

*falling in love
all over again*

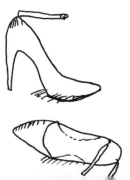

going barefoot

a good night's sleep

a new challenge

a well-earned compliment

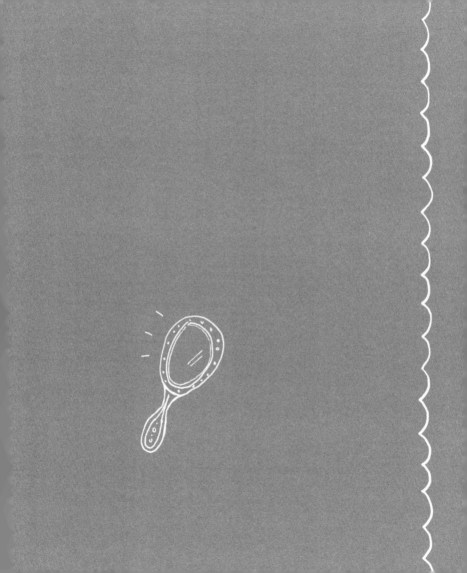

being part of
something good

surprise parties

splashing in puddles

the first true day
of spring

a massage

ladybugs

four-leaf clovers

sudden inspiration

small victories

shooting stars

a phone call
from an old friend,
just when you need it

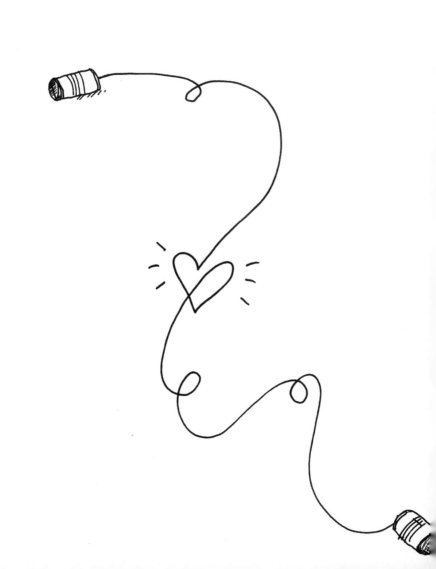

a favorite song ♪♫
♪♫ on the radio

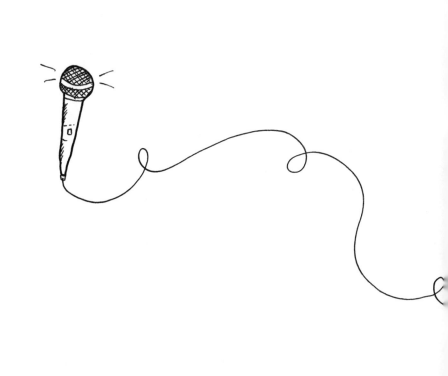

{ feeling healthy }

knowing you've
done your best

free afternoons

fruit trees in bloom

fresh whipped cream

picnics

summer rainstorms

glitter

the sound of the ocean

fresh air

hot coffee on
a camping trip

the right words
at the right time

penny candy

the smell of
freshly cut grass

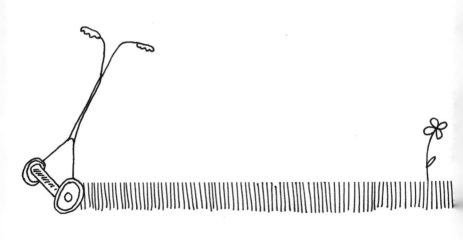

helping someone in need

reliving a wonderful memory

{ sand between
your toes }

berry - picking

farmers' markets

giving thanks

open minds

finding something to be passionate about

- - - - - - - - - - - -

the light at sunset

the perfect peach

an unexpected package
in the mail

♡ feeling appreciated ♡

seeing someone
else's smile

a friend who's
willing to listen

running through
a sprinkler

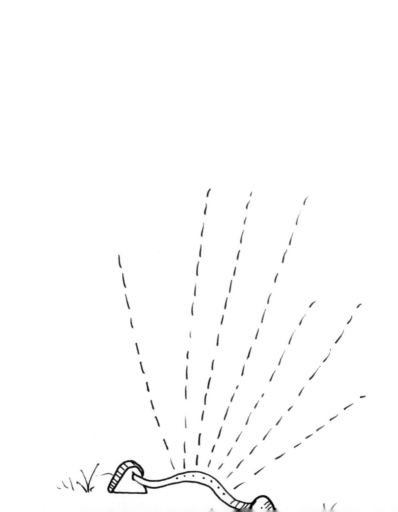

a sudden fit of the giggles

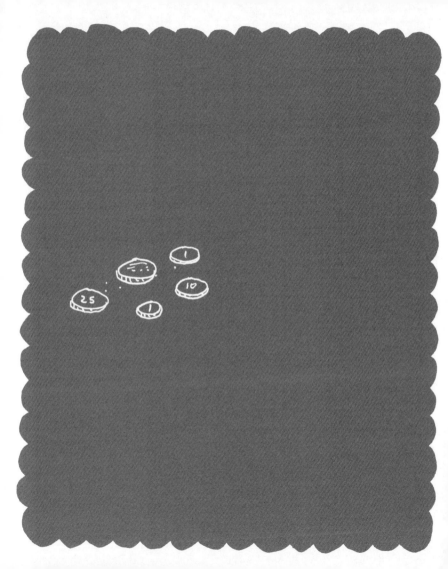

finding forgotten
pocket change

generosity

optimism

↑

a great goal to work for

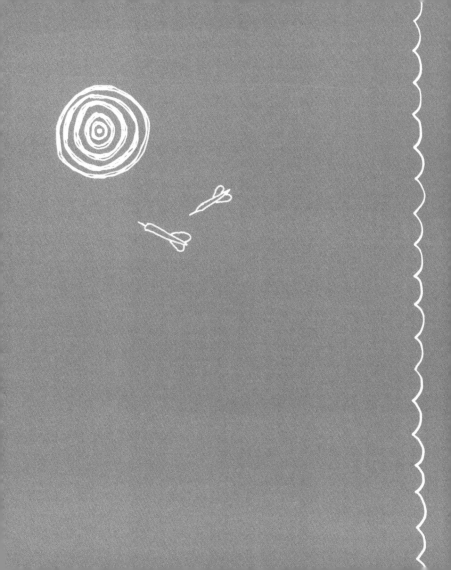

a new friend

things that are
meant to be shared

porch swings

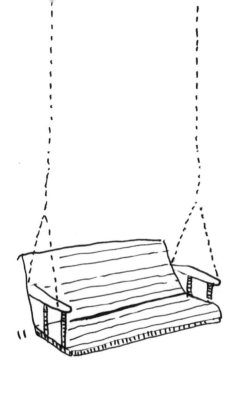

seeing newlyweds

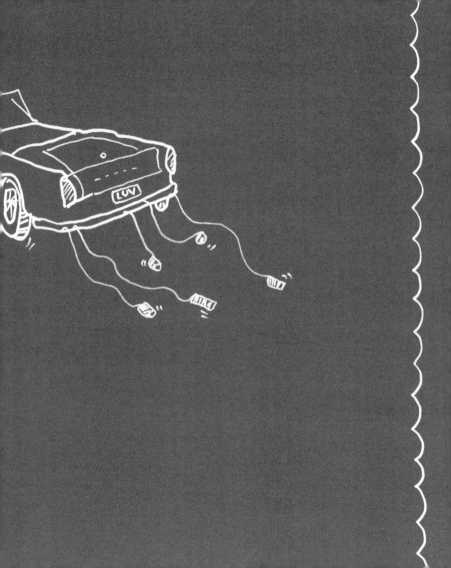

crisp fall mornings

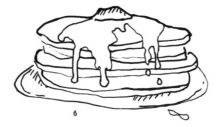

real maple syrup

listening to rain
on the roof

children's laughter

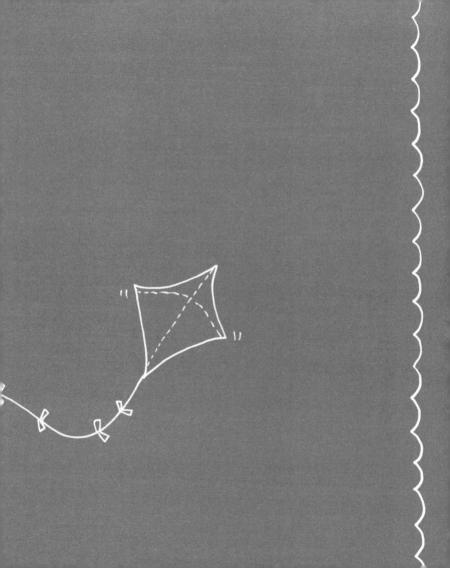

tandem bicycles

blowing bubbles

drawings done in
sidewalk chalk

brunch with friends

holding hands

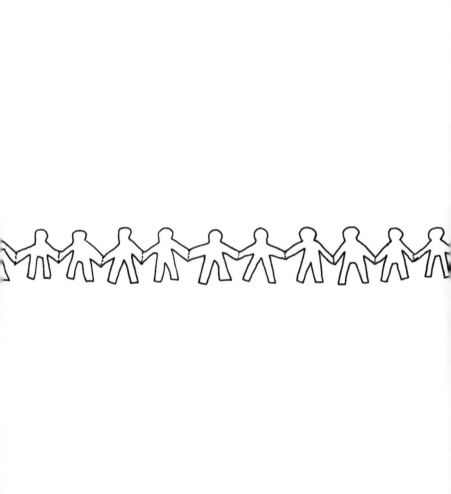

music playing through
an open window

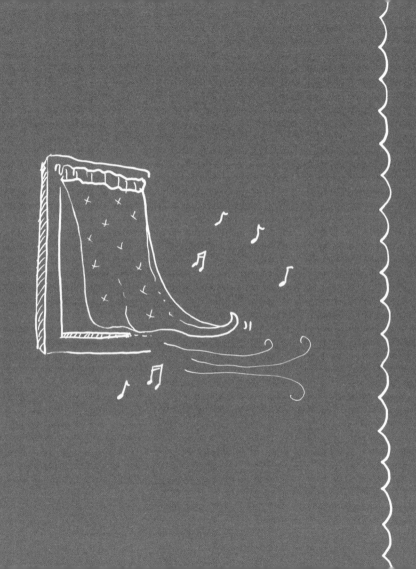

tree swings

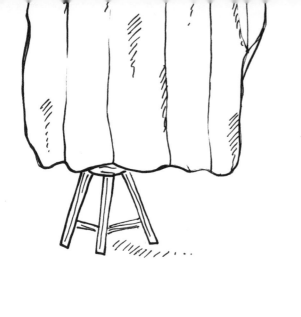

=: photo booths :=

a long, hot bath

making something from scratch

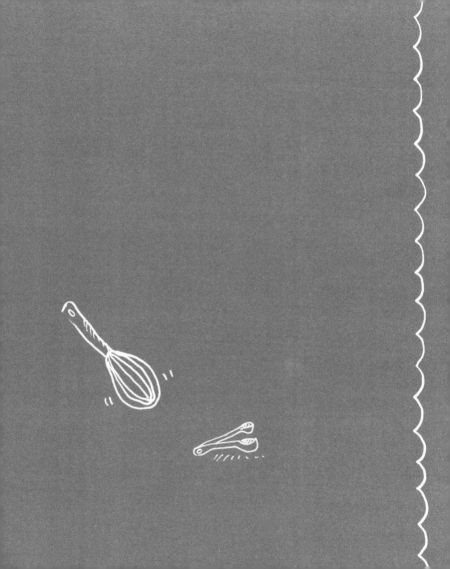

{ recycling }

nice neighbors

being there for
someone else

doing something
to be proud of

brilliant autumn leaves

{ trick or treaters }

hot buttered popcorn

~~~~~~~~~~

a new box of crayons

~~~~~~~~~~

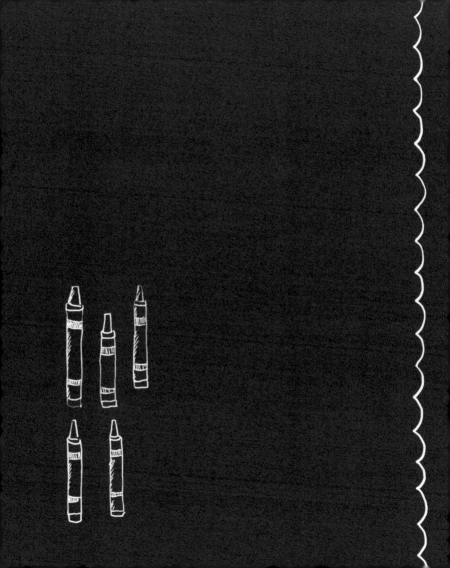

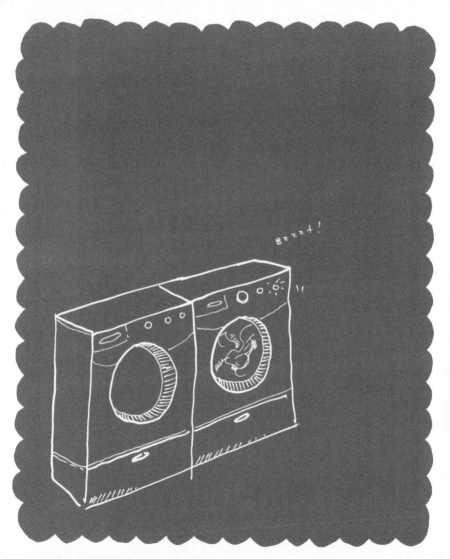

towels hot from the dryer

puppies

happy accidents

the ripple effect of a
simple act of kindness

"𝓑𝓑 𝓑𝓑"

working to build a
better world

- -dancing - -

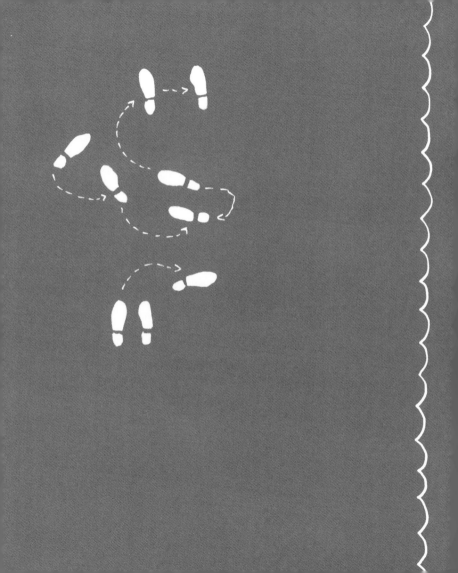

an elderly couple
in love

taking the scenic route

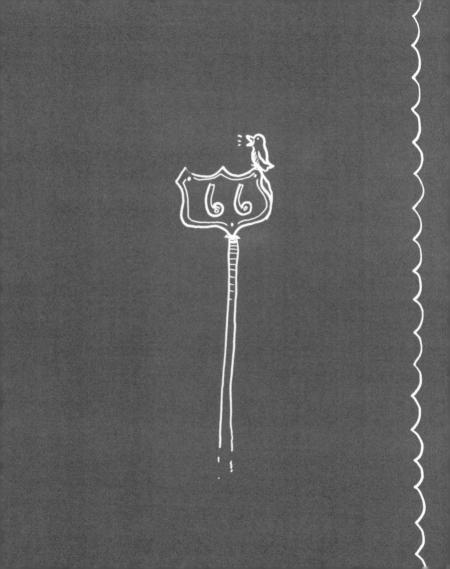

making progress

watching a reunion
at the airport

||||||||||||||||||||···.

—— ♡ ——

holidays with family

———————

cocoa with marshmallows

helping someone
build a snowman

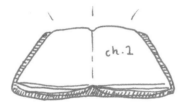

turning the pages of
a crisp new book

a goodnight kiss

the smell of an
evergreen tree

birds at the feeder

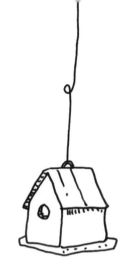

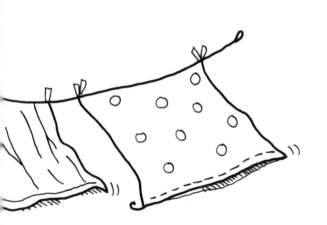

clean sheets

waking up to
new - fallen snow

What makes YOU smile ?

_____

_____

_____

_____